DESTINED TO INSPIRE

DYLAN R. MELOFSKY

authorHOUSE®

AuthorHouse™
1663 Liberty Drive
Bloomington, IN 47403
www.authorhouse.com
Phone: 833-262-8899

Published by AuthorHouse 10/19/2020

ISBN: 978-1-6655-0518-5 (sc)
ISBN: 978-1-6655-0517-8 (e)

Library of Congress Control Number: 2020920863

Print information available on the last page.

Any people depicted in stock imagery provided by Getty Images are models,
and such images are being used for illustrative purposes only.
Certain stock imagery © Getty Images.

This book is printed on acid-free paper.

CONTENTS

PREFACE

I want to thank you personally for taking the time out of your life
to read what I have written. Before I concluded that I would write
this, I didn't give a lot of thought toward detailed specifics on what
I was going to do with my life from any aspect. I had just a normal
routine day to day which I didn't realize was being stuck in the system.
However, a close friend and I have been talking daily regarding deep
subjects about our life and purpose. Over the past few months, it started
to register in me that life has real meaning when you can unplug from
the consistent negativity that surrounds all of us. I watched a couple
of videos on YouTube and read 'The Secret' by Rhonda Byrne. That's
when the idea to write this book came to me, and unlike every other
idea that has come and gone, I wanted to take full advantage of the
opportunity to get this accomplished. I needed this book more than
you will ever know. I hope that it will help you as much as it helped me.

CHAPTER 1

---*⚙*---

START

Start: to use a particular point, action, or circumstance as an opening for a course of action.

HERE WE GO. THIS IS NEW for me as reading something like this might be new to you. I've never written a book or even inclined to do so, but here I go. With everything that is, always has a beginning.

"Every accomplishment starts with the decision to try." -John F. Kennedy

It takes a lot of effort to go against the grain for the first time in any circumstance. Starting anything new can seem very challenging. It can be filled with doubt, confusion, and anxiety. We live our lives in a world where we are taught that doing just enough is enough. We may get an idea to start something like a project around the house, a new hobby that seems intriguing, or even a business venture, but how many times does it fall through? How many times have you given up? To make it clearer, how many times have you given up on yourself?

I know firsthand how it feels to give up. I would go through phases where I would be captivated by a promising idea or something else that I valued to be entertaining for a couple of weeks or sometimes months, but eventually, I would abandon the idea. I would convince myself that it wasn't worth my time, or that I had better things I could be doing rather than pursuing that new idea. I only quit because I was afraid to keep going. I was afraid of failure. I was afraid of the way people may view my efforts.

Although starting is the first step, for most, it's the hardest thing to do when they want to change. Deep down we all want to change something about ourselves. It could be mentally, physically, emotionally, or even financially. In reality, we are constantly growing. Even though we may hit a specific age where we believe the growing process to be over, it never truly ends.

"The beginning is the most important part of the work." -Plato

3 years ago, I weighed 230 pounds. I'm not a tall guy by any means whatsoever so 230 pounds is pretty overweight for me. It came to a point where I couldn't bend over to tie my shoes without my stomach getting in the way. I looked at myself one day in the mirror and said, "I don't want to look like this anymore." I set a goal for myself to be 165 lbs. I had to start a new process. I had to change. I had to give up my old mindset of junk food and soft drinks and start on a new path of healthy food and exercise. A path where I would have to push myself into trying something new. A path where I had to eat baked chicken instead of chips. A path where I had to run hundreds of miles instead of sitting on the couch. A path where I would doubt myself and eventually give up. About 6 months later, I lost 35 lbs. but then stopped. Sure, I looked and felt better, but I gave up. I achieved so much, yet I still gave up. Why? I was accomplishing what I set my mind to do, so why did I stop? Maybe it was because I had to start working twice as hard to lose more weight. Maybe it was questions of doubt and uncertainty that would creep into my mind "what if I truly can't do it?" "Do I have what it takes?" Either way, I stopped trying to lose weight and gave up. I gave up when I had already been seeing firsthand the accomplishments that I had been achieving since my starting point. That was it; I was done. I didn't consider or even think about striving to achieve my sought-after goal until about a year ago. I had the desire to start again but this time I wouldn't give up. I wouldn't give in. I was 195 lbs. and reignited my goal to be 165 lbs. I picked up right where I left off and in 2 months, I hit my goal.

"The right way to get started is to quit talking and begin doing." -Walt Disney

I used to mention to some of my friends that I had found purpose to start something with no true intention to ever really start. They were just ideas coming to me and disappearing just as soon as I would get them out my mouth.

If you have a desire to start a passion, to start a hobby, to start writing, to start a business, DO IT! Most people will tell you that "you've got better things to do than that" or "You know you can't do it". I'm here to tell you, go for it. Pursue it with all of your heart. Block out the negativity with hope. Trust in yourself. Believe in yourself. You DO have what it takes. What do you have to lose? Start now! You CAN and you WILL accomplish it. All you have to do is take the first step.

"Start by doing what is necessary, then do what's possible, and suddenly you are doing the impossible." -Saint Francis of Assisi

If you look at whatever you plan on starting as being overwhelming or too difficult, then that is exactly what it will be. You will lose the desire to begin because you've already made up in your mind that it's going to be too hard to strive for. If you look at it instead as either a challenge or a fun activity that you truly enjoy, then it no longer will seem to be this overcast shadow of uncertainty or dread. The process will be enjoyable instead of something to be fearful of. You will love every minute of it. Think about today as the first day of your process. Your beginning to your story. Don't let doubt creep into your mind to keep you from starting your story. Go after it, now is the time! You are the director of your movie, the author of your book. How exciting!

Every idea that comes to mind, every feeling of creativity that you want to express, you owe it to yourself and the people around you. What are the things that make you happy? What are the ambitions you've thought about seeking? What are you truly passionate about? Only you know who you truly are, and what you truly want out of life. Only you know what you want to change about yourself or your surroundings. You have the power to do so, and it all starts with the first step. No one else can take the step for you. Only you can decide which path you will take. One way or the other you are heading in a direction. The question becomes, is the path that you are on a path you paved for yourself or is it a path that has been paved for you by someone else, for their liking? The path of your destiny ultimately is yours for the taking.

Something for me that is very encouraging is writing this book itself. As I'm letting the ideas come to my head for the next sentence I write, I feel this warmth coming over me telling me that I'm making a difference in the world. I'm uplifting people to chase what belongs to them. To inspire direction. To help someone find purpose if they've lost it. To lose fear if they've found it. I'm creating history. I'm writing a book. I'm accomplishing it. Anytime you're starting something new it's always good to celebrate the little wins. How comforting it is to build yourself up.

Every paragraph, every sentence, every word I write is a little win for me to be proud of. Focusing on fear, doubt, and worry will only hold me back from accomplishing this goal. My passion is to make a difference positively not only for myself but for you, the reader. To keep the commitment and determination to show you and myself that I can do this. If I can accomplish this, then you can accomplish whatever you set your mind to. Don't be stagnant. Let your light shine and let your life flow in the direction you see fit.

> *"Faith is taking the first step even when you don't see the whole staircase."* - Martin Luther King Jr.

I don't know what will come from this book, how many eyes it will reach or how many lives it will touch. But I know in my heart this is beneficial in the growth and belief in one's self. I am on a journey and I'm dictating what's happening. I'm deciding to start this change.

How do we begin? How do we start something new? First and foremost, you have to have confidence in yourself to start something new. To look in the mirror and say to yourself, "Today is where I begin this process." "Today is where I will start the change." "I know that I can do it." Right now, as I am writing this book, I'm erasing all doubts that I will fail. I will not focus on what others might think. I will not give up on the story I'm telling. For as I'm writing this for you, the reader, I'm writing this for myself.

This is not the end; far from it. This is only the beginning.

CHAPTER 2

·•◦❋◦•·

DREAM

Dream: a cherished aspiration, ambition, or ideal.

I N ALL HONESTY, I NEVER HAD a dream as a child or even as a teenager. I loved watching comedies so I would find myself impersonating Jim Carey or Ben Stiller from some of their movies. I guess you could say I wanted to be an actor, but it's not something I constantly thought about or ever took seriously. I loved rap and rock music, so I also imagined being a rapper or a rock star. I thought about how cool it would be to stand in front of thousands of people pumping up the crowd and feeling iconic, but once again, I never took it seriously because that just seemed ludicrous. I never really felt like dreaming was something I was destined for. I assumed getting a job working 9-5 trying to beat the traffic daily was all that there was for me.

> *"Every great dream begins with a dreamer always remember,*
> *you have within you the strength, the patience, and the passion*
> *to reach for the stars and change the world."* - Harriet Tubman

One of my closest and dearest friends has a dream of becoming a full-time musician, and as long as I've known him, he's been chasing it. He is a phenomenal guitarist with an incredible talent for writing music and coming up with melodies. To say the least, his passion is his music. We could be in the middle of a conversation and a melody hits him and he would quickly pull his phone out, open his microphone app and record himself humming a tune that comes to him.

I told my friend that I don't have a dream. I don't have a drive for anything like that. Dreaming just wasn't me. I tried to think of something that I'm good at and love to do, but I just couldn't do it. I predetermined that I didn't have the drive or ambition to start or chase anything that I couldn't see in my mind's eye.

Eventually, I started reading self-help books, meditating and watched YouTube videos on the law of attraction. I was doing everything I could to find my calling in life, and if I couldn't, I could say I tried and at the very least I would be a better person by applying the things that I would learn in the books and videos about self-awareness, how our brains work, and most importantly, the law of attraction. I read a book called *"The Secret"* by Rhonda Byrne and that's when it hit me, so I started writing this book. I've always loved talking to people, getting to know individuals on a personal level. To relate and comprehend how people are feeling and finding ways that I can help them in any way that I can. To love and cherish the bonds of friendships and to be genuine in caring about people's feelings. That's when I knew that I wanted to be someone that can inspire and lead by example to push people to chase their dreams.

> *"Have the courage to follow your heart and intuition. They somehow know what you truly want to become."* - Steve Jobs

As I'm writing the second chapter of this book, I'm using everything that I have at my disposal to pursue my dreams. My dreams of helping you mentally to understand how truly important you are. To show you by example that I'm going after this with all of my heart. To push myself beyond my limitations and write this book. To not waste my time with anything other than what's truly important. To not waste any more time than isn't promised. My dreams are coming to fruition every single day as I continue on this journey of self-love and inspiration.

> *"Imagination is everything. It is the preview of life's coming attractions."* -Albert Einstein

As I've come to grasp the idea of having a dream and how I found what mine is, I not only ask, but beg you to understand that if you feel that you don't have a dream, you are wrong. You just haven't recognized it yet. You are a special and unique individual with a purpose. You have a gift that no one else has. Don't discredit your talents before you've even given them a chance. I know this from experience. I genuinely felt that I was not special in any way shape or form. I was just another worker bee that could be replaced at the drop of a hat. Someone who would be forgotten once they were gone. I'm here to tell you that it is not how I will go out. I will leave a lasting mark on this world. I will reach those who doubt their true potential in life. Those who will shape the future of this planet. Those with dreams and aspirations that only they could see themselves conquering. I owe my belief in them the same as they owe their gifts to this world. Just as the great dreamers of the past had visions of a future, ones they only imagined in their minds and created with their hearts, so do I and so do you. We are alive with purpose and meaning for all of humanity.

"All that we are is the result of what we have thought." -Buddha

Some of the greatest minds in history had dreams that changed the course of history forever. Thomas Edison, Orville and Wilbur Wright, William Shakespeare, Beethoven, Andrew Carnegie, and Henry Ford. The list of these influential shapers of our world can go on and on. They all have one thing in common: they did it with their dreams. They didn't let their limitations, or anyone's opinion deter them from chasing their dreams. You are no different from them. They were just people like you and me today. You have a brain just as they did that consciously and subconsciously creates your reality whether you accept it or not. Your thought processes dictate everything you have done and will ever do. You had to decide to work where you do. You had to decide which shirt you were going to wear today. You're going to decide the next restaurant you are visiting. The decisions you make impact your life on both small and large scales.

Think about where you will be in 10 years. Are you happy where you are in your life right now? Are you content with your atmosphere? It can be your financial dependence, it can be your physique, the people you surround yourself with or as simple as your mental disposition to yourself and the world around you. When you realize that you have the authority to not only change your circumstances but can create them, you can create your happiness. You can create anything, literally ANYTHING. Even if it seems farfetched or completely out of reach, it's not. The impossible is only impossible because we haven't made it possible yet.

"Nothing is impossible, the word itself says "I'm possible." - Audrey Hepburn

As I continue to write this book it is constantly reminding me of how this is beneficial not only for you, the reader but also for me, the author. I am finding much joy in being able to encourage you just as I have encouraged myself to find my purpose on how I can impact humanity in such a fulfilling way. To reach you on a deeper level than I ever thought I possibly could. To push myself beyond what I would view as the limit of my capabilities. To dissipate whatever doubts or negativity that comes. As you see firsthand that I'm achieving my dream, here's where I challenge you. Here's where I push you, to motivate you to find your purpose, for you to chase your dreams with all of your heart and acknowledge that you have a unique vision that you will make happen in your own beautiful way.

CHAPTER 3

BELIEVE

Believe: accept (something) as true; feel sure of the truth.

I CAN'T LIE TO YOU, BELIEVING CAN be tricky, especially when it involves believing in yourself. I can name countless times when I didn't believe. One belief that comes to mind was the belief that couldn't go to college. I assumed I would never have high enough grades to pass or that I would never have enough money to afford it. I didn't have in mind what I wanted to pursue as a career anyways. I believed there was not a sliver of a chance I could ever make it. I made that decision when I was a sophomore in high school, and guess who didn't go to college because of that lack of faith? Me.

"It is a lack of faith that makes people afraid of meeting challenges, and I believed in myself." -Muhammad Ali

Believing is the groundwork of where all things are possible. Without it, all hope, passion, and desire are non-existent. Why would we do anything without belief? Believing in something that comes easy to some and hard for others. Looking at belief on smaller scales of everyday life to see how I can apply it to big ones has helped me with grasping the concept. Take for instance when we are in our cars driving to work. We don't know if we will have a blowout on the way there, get into an accident or whatever else may happen. But that doesn't stop us from driving there, every day. That is belief. That is believing we will make it without proof we will. We believe every day without consciously knowing we do.

"Just believe in yourself. Even if you don't, pretend that you do and at some point, you will." - Venus Williams

I'm using this belief structure to continue my journey. I'm using belief to write this book. As I've said before, I don't know what's to come of this book, but here I go, filling pages with the words that come to mind and channeling it right out of my fingertips with belief. I believe this will leave a legacy in the pages. I believe it will be a lasting impression on you, and a never forgettable effort to achieve greatness. As I write this, I think of all of the future readers that I would be letting down if I didn't express my belief in them. All the people that need this belief. I know how it feels to not believe in myself. I altered my path forever by not believing in who I truly am. That changes today. Today I believe in who I am and what I can accomplish. Yes, there will be times where thoughts will come into my mind, telling me that I should stop trying, to let up just a tad. I can hear the doubt now "You don't have what it takes." "You're not going to reach anyone." "You don't seriously believe you can write a book, do you?" I hear the uncertainty. I hear the doubt. I WILL NOT GIVE IN. I will not let myself stop what I've started. I will not give up on you. I will not give up on my purpose. I will achieve greatness. I will reach people. I will inspire you. I will believe in myself.

"Believe you can and your halfway there." -Theodore Roosevelt.

I can see the people that I'm influencing. I'm influencing them to believe in themselves. That's what keeps pushing me. It keeps this drive in me to go after it with all I have in me. I want to change this world for the good. To see others, take a stand for what they believe in. To see everyone believing in one another. For people to not question their intuition but feed into it. To have faith and believe in whatever their spirituality calls on them to do.

"The brain simply believes in what you tell it most. And what you tell it about you, it will create. It has no choice." - Shad Helmstetter

Something that I've gotten into the habit of is talking to myself at any given opportunity. When I'm all by myself to just give myself an extra kick of motivation I'll close my eyes and just talk. It can be as simple as "I love you" or "I'm proud of you". Those simple little nudges go a long way when it comes to believing in yourself. It starts taking root and eventually you start genuinely believing what you're saying. You can close your eyes to do it, make eye contact with yourself in the mirror, or do whatever you feel works for you. You could even record yourself speaking a positive message and listen to it later. It does not matter how you go about this. The point is to get your message to take hold in your subconscious, and it will happen if you are repetitive in it. Without realizing it you will eventually start believing what you are telling yourself. Make it a daily habit to believe in yourself. Believe you can achieve your sought-after vision. Your subconscious is where your belief has to take hold before you can make it into a reality.

> *"If you can't fly then run if you can't run then walk if you can't walk then crawl, but whatever you do, you have to keep moving forward."* - Martin Luther King Jr.

Never look back at anything that can throw you off of your flow of belief. If you just keep pressing, you will accomplish your desired achievement. It can be easy to pull the "woe is me" card, bring yourself down and feel sorry for yourself, but that is detrimental for your mentality. Instead of looking toward your past trials or failures, look toward the future of all of the endless possibilities that lie in store for you. The best part is, you have all the power to choose your course in whichever direction you want to go. Your belief dictates where you will go.

"Believe in yourself when nobody else does." -Mary J. Blige

I've told various people that I'm writing a book. Some look at me with a quirky smirk that says, "really dude?" "You've got to be kidding right?". Some are a little more optimistic about my ideas, about what I'm writing, and ask me what I plan to do with it once I'm finished. Last, there are the few that truly believe in my vision and see how this can help the world.

All 3 categories of people are in belief. One way or the other, they believe. The first group believes I'll quit a couple of sentences or paragraphs in. They believe that I will delete it all from existence and continue to let the world pass me by. The second group believes it has the potential to be a good book and can see it in a bookstore. The third group takes hold of the idea not from the perspective of a reader but from the perspective of a person who has ideas themselves. They have ideas that will shape their reality around them. Those that believe in this book will not only change the world in the future, but they are already changing the world around them as they read it.

> *"Faith that it's not always in your hands or things don't always go the way you planned, but you have to have faith that there is a plan for you, and you must follow your heart and believe in yourself no matter what."* - Martina McBride

At the beginning of this chapter, I was lost on where I was going to go with the subject of belief. I had no plan on how I was going to convey this chapter or how I could use it for myself in my personal growth. However, I realized that, after all, I am one of the people in the third group. I believe this book will change the world. I believe it will impact people in whatever way they can perceive. The possibilities are endless when belief has been instilled. I believe this book will cause people to trust in themselves, the same way that I trust in myself to continue writing it.

> *"My mindset is to go out there and be confident, believe in yourself, visualizing success and visualizing plays you're going to make...."* - Saquan Barkley

Will writing this book help me go after what I believe in? For me, the answer isn't a straightforward "yes" or "no". This is an instance where I can't say for certain that it will or will not help. This is the point where I have to believe and have faith that it already is helping me. I have to believe that it is helping you.

CHAPTER 4

—•❋•—

GOALS

Goals: The object(s) of a person's ambition or effort; an aim for the desired result.

GOALS WERE SOMETHING I'VE ALWAYS HEARD about. Having goals was always something that you were supposed to set for yourself. However, I didn't care about that at all. When I was young, I simply went to school, came home, played video games, and then went to sleep. As a teenager, I did the same thing. As an adult? You guessed it, I went to work, came home played video games, ate, and went to sleep. It has taken me over 25 years to understand how important goals are to have.

*"You should set goals beyond your reach, so you always have something to live for." -*Ted Turner

Losing weight was the first real goal I set for myself. Although I didn't know it at the time, that first goal was something that would stay in my subconscious forever. It was from that point on where I would start setting goals for myself. I didn't think anything of how vital the setting of that one goal would be for my mentality until I reached the weight I desired. After I achieved my goal, it's like a fire was lit in me to set new goals for myself. Once I achieved the next goal, I was excited to achieve another. Before long I was addicted to the challenges I was setting for myself.

*"Don't be a spectator, don't let life pass you by." -*Lou Holtz

Have you ever heard of a bucket list? If you haven't it's a list of things that you want to do or achieve before you die. Lou Holtz, a hall of fame college football coach, created his bucket list at the age of 28. In that list, he came up with 107 goals. Those goals included meeting the pope, being a guest on the Tonight Show, coaching the Notre Dame Football team, and landing a plane on an aircraft carrier. Fast forward to today, Lou Holtz has accomplished 102 of his 107 goals. Let that sink in for a minute.

"If you want to be happy, set a goal that commands your thoughts, liberates your energy, and inspires your hopes." -Andrew Carnegie

Since I've started writing this book not only has it been helping me in my own life, but I've been able to express the way it makes me feel towards the people around me. I've been working my current job for almost 5 years now. Some people I've come to know through those years, but there are others that I might know by name that I haven't approached and introduced myself to. I set a goal one morning to try to speak and shake everyone's hand that I would just so happen to run into at work. I did this for a couple of days and then I set a new goal for myself. Next, I went out of my way to see who I don't see regularly that works there and introduced myself. Soon, I accomplished that so, what's next? Then, I began to shake their hands, hug them, and let them know that I'm thankful to see them today. Since I've started this process things are different. They are expecting to see me now regularly. They are expecting me to make my way to where they are, hug them, show them that I care about them, and end the small conversations with "I'm so thankful to have seen you." The impact that it has had on my life couldn't be more rewarding. I don't have a clue as to if they are having a good day, a bad day if they're happy, or depressed. All I know is that one way or the other I'm accomplishing these new goals I'm setting for myself.

"By recording your dreams and goals on paper, you set in motion the process of becoming the person you want to be. Put your future in good hands-your own." -Mark Victor Hansen

15

As I continue to set these goals for myself, I ask you to do the same. Don't set just one goal, set as many as you possibly can. As you start accomplishing them, you will begin to have more confidence in your ability to accomplish the tougher goals on your list. You will start doing the things you want to do, and you will start becoming the person you want to be. There is no limit to how big or small the goals can be. That's the beauty in it. You can decide your life's course with the goals you set.

> *"One way to keep momentum going is to have constantly greater goals."* -Michael Korda

Momentum is an extremely powerful tool when it comes to setting and achieving goals. In the beginning, when you first start to think about a goal to write down it can be a challenge, but once you have a goal written down then another one comes to mind. Then, before long, you've accumulated a hefty list in front of you. When you first get on a bicycle, you have to put the most effort into those first few pedals before the momentum catches up and it's all smooth sailing from there. Just as riding a bike, achieving your goals is no different. Sure, it takes quite a bit of effort to start the process but once you start, it's like you can't stop.

> *"The thing about goals is that living without them is a lot more fun, in the short run. It seems to me, though, that the people who get things done, who lead, who grow and who make an impact those people have goals."* -Seth Godin

It's taken me 25 years to set life-changing goals for myself. Goals that will take me to places I only dreamed of. Goals of inspiration, personal growth, and abundance. Have you decided to make a bucket list? What exciting goals have you thought of while reading this chapter? As I continue to write, I am showing you and myself that I am not only setting goals, but I'm accomplishing them.

CHAPTER 5

---•◦❈◦•---

HUMILITY

Humble: A modest or low view of one's importance; humbleness

N O ONE EVER THINKS TOO LOWLY of themselves, do they? No one is ever wrong. "No need to tell me anything, I already know it all." "Yeah, I know how great I am at everything I do." Do you know anyone like that? Are you like that? I know I was.

"A great man is always willing to be little." -Ralph Waldo Emerson

People love getting compliments. For me, when someone complimented me, I would let it take hold of my whole demeanor and it would impact me in the worst way possible. I would get a sense of arrogance from compliments. Instead of just appreciating the compliments as they came and not giving them a second thought, I would harbor them. They took over me. I truly felt I was better than everyone else, and that is a terrible mentality to be in.

"Humility is not thinking less of yourself; it's thinking of yourself less." -C.S. Lewis

Once you get so hung up on yourself and feel so high on how great you are there's only one place to go from there, down. I found myself in a deep depression where I felt that I had no purpose. An existential crisis if you will. However, the more you mature, the more the scales completely flip. I went from thinking that I was the best to thinking I was the worst. It was that moment that changed my life forever. I felt so unsure of myself. For acting as someone that I wasn't. I was so embarrassed by how I allowed this arrogance to almost destroy my life. I lost the desire to live. I had to find my will again, through humility.

"Life is a long lesson in humility." -James M. Barrie

With humility, I found my purpose, to build others up. To use confidence to reach people in ways I never thought I could and teach them to believe in themselves. I'm no better than anyone else. We are all just people, and we live our lives by our circumstances. Regardless of your race, religion, political views, sexual orientation or financial status, we should show a humble attitude in all facets of life. If you are at the grocery store and someone is behind you, why not let them go ahead of you? What's the rush? If you're on the interstate and someone wants to get over, why not slow down a little to let them over? What about owning up to something you know you've done wrong? Why not apologize to someone you've wronged. Why not help someone when they need it? Humility is the key to a happy, stress-free life.

"Humility will open more doors than arrogance ever will."
Zig Ziglar

As I ponder on humility and how it affects my life, I realize that it's scary to not know all of the answers, which is why we don't want to listen. Apologizing to people is intimidating because, in our minds, it shows weakness. It's terrifying to self-evaluate because change means being different. We like the comfort of knowing what we know and having all of the answers. Staying right where we are because we know it's safe. In my life, I have wrecked friendships that I will never be able to salvage. I have burnt bridges by being the one responsible for lighting the match. I've said hurtful things to people who cared for me. I have regrets in life just as you might. But you must be able to step back, recognize your faults, change your attitude, shift your awareness, realize that you're not that same person, and most importantly forgive freely, most importantly forgiving yourself.

"If history teaches us anything, it teaches us humility." -Gordon S. Woods

It takes humility to write this book. I'm opening up myself to whoever reads this book. Am I afraid of who sees this book might think it's bad or a waste of time? The answer is NO. I want you to understand how being humble is extremely important in self-growth. By my reasoning with you about who I am, how I view my attitude of the past, and what I want my attitude to be right now, I hope that it will inspire you to not be afraid to look in the mirror and say to yourself "I might need to work on....". It doesn't matter what you choose, but I bet you can find one thing you want to change. I don't know what it is that could be bothering you now, or what will bother you in the future, but as you apply humility, the way you see things and the way people view you start to change. All of your stress melts away when you can shift your focus to humility.

"In a gentle way, you can shake the world." -Mahatma Gandhi

I remember wanting to fit in everywhere I would go. I wanted to be a cool dude and to be liked by those who everyone wanted to be around. I wanted people to notice me. I wanted people to wish they were around me. This mindset was arrogant. I copied the behaviors of the people around me that were popular because I assumed that was the way you were supposed to be. I lied to myself and others that I was a person whom I wasn't. Because of my behavior, I had friends, but they were fake friends, just as I was. I've been applying what I've read in the past, what I'm reading now, and what I'm writing, and it has helped me grow into who I am. By showing my true colors without the fear of being judged, people accept me for who I am. By showing who I am, people show me who they are. By being who I am will make people hate me or love me. There is no middle ground because I'm not being half of who I am. I am 100% the Dylan I was destined to be and no one else. The ones who love me are the ones who are supposed to love me. The ones who hate me are the ones who are supposed to hate me. Maybe this identity that I'm striving for is overbearing to some. They might think I'm trying to impress someone, or that I'm trying to pull one over on them. They might think it's all an act. I can see where they are coming from. It's different from anything they've ever witnessed. Either way, whether they look at me like I'm disingenuous or genuine, it's making them think. If the people aren't viewing your efforts with an accepting attitude it could have to do with people that have betrayed them in the past and took their kindness for weakness. The fact that they are rejecting you might even mean they didn't get the affection they needed in their upbringing. Either way, showing them that you love and appreciate them is still a good act because you've shown them something that they may have been lacking their whole life. The ones that think I am genuine make it abundantly obvious. I went up to someone and did my usual intro to one person, and it made an impact on him for the rest of that day. I was taking the trash out to the dumpster at work, and he walked up to me and said, "You know what you did this morning meant a lot to me, I needed to hear some encouraging words." Something as little as "Hello" or "I'm thankful to see you" can change someone's mood for the entire day. A simple act of humility goes a long way. I don't have anything to gain from sharing these true feelings. The only thing that I stand to gain is the happiness I create by sharing happiness in my own life and other's lives around me. Making small exchanges might seem insignificant at first, but I could be planting seeds to make people realize it's not so hard to be different- to be unique- to be who you are. Those little displays of humility show you care.

Opening up about yourself to others can be intimidating because you could be afraid of how people might react, but to me, it's exciting. I'm able to view life from a different point of view, realizing how important every moment is. We aren't promised tomorrow. So, why not be exactly who you are at this moment? Why not be a compassionate human being?

"You must be the change you wish to see in the world." -Mahatma Gandhi

Humility to most is an eye-opener. I would have never guessed that I would put so much of myself into this. As the chapters go by, each makes me realize how much I needed to apply these principles to my own life, especially this chapter.

CHAPTER 6

—•⊛•—

LEADERSHIP

Leadership: The action of leading a group of people or an organization

W**HAT DOES IT TAKE TO BE** a leader? If I'm going to follow someone, I want to know which direction they are going. What's their motive? What examples are they setting? Do they have goals? If so, how serious do they take them? Before I follow anyone, I have to truly believe in what they believe. There would be no reason for me to waste my time otherwise. A leader can't just say they are going to do something, they have to prove that they can. Regarding any aspect of leadership, the most important thing is that they are supportive and willing to do what is necessary. A good leader puts others above themselves.

*"Before you are a leader success is about growing yourself. When you become a leader, success is all about growing others." -*Jack Welch

A good leader sets examples that others want to follow. We all have been followers of some kind. The people we are around influence our behavior, attitude, likes and dislikes. The people we associate with impact our behavior without us even realizing it. If you surround yourself with people who complain and have a defeatist attitude, you might not grab hold to the trait at first, but over time, you slowly start to adopt it. If you surround yourself with people that are very polite and well-mannered, then you will act with a courteous well-rounded attitude.

> *"A leader is one who knows the way, goes the way, and shows the way."* John C. Maxwell

So, let me take a step back and look at myself for a second. If I plan on being a good leader than I need to learn from those who were good leaders. Mahatma Gandhi, Abraham Lincoln, George Washington, Martin Luther King Jr. What made them great leaders? What did they have in common? They wholeheartedly believed in what they stood for, without any doubt. They sought the truth, placed courage over fear, had empathy toward themselves and others. So, I ask myself this important question: are you going to be a great leader? Where there is a will, there is a way.

> *"A genuine leader is not a searcher for a consensus but a molder of consensus."* -Martin Luther King Jr.

To follow in the footsteps of great leaders takes courage to make a transition. I'm having to make a change within myself to even be able to comprehend what it means to lead. These great figures left the groundwork not just for me, but for you. You can be a good leader. Even if you say there's no way you can lead, you can.

> *"Leaders don't create followers; they create more leaders."* -Tom Peters

I want to be a leader that inspires. Every day I'm trying to be the best leader for myself internally, to lead externally. I want to change the world, to erase fear, and inspire hope. A hope that we can accomplish the impossible. Since we are in the information age we have at the touch of our fingertips all that we need to accomplish PEACE. So many have tried and failed in the past for peace so how can it be done? Peace isn't something that exists in the external world. You can't walk around with a bag full of peace. It has to be implemented within to be expressed outwardly. It all starts with one. I am working every day to be the best person that I can be for myself and the people around me. I'm doing it not only for me but for us. It doesn't matter what stage in your life you're in, young, old, rich, poor, stable, or unstable you can always rise above. Together we will rise.

> *"Every time you have to speak, you are auditioning for leadership."* -James Humes

CHAPTER 7

POSITIVE

Positive: constructive, optimistic, or confident.

GROWING UP I LIVED IN A lot of different places with different circumstances. At one point my mother worked 3 different jobs to pay the bills, so I didn't see her a lot. I never even met my father; my mother has 2 pictures of him when they were together. So, I've seen his face, but I've never heard his voice. I don't know what his personality is or what things he enjoys doing in his free time. When he found out my mom was pregnant with me, he tried to get her to have an abortion. When she didn't, he went back home to his wife and 3 kids. I have 2 older sisters and an older brother that I've never met, and I doubt they know I exist. My mom did the best she could with the hand she was dealt. To make it easy on her and myself, I lived with some people my mom thought she knew well. However, they weren't very good at taking care of me. I recall kids in school making fun of me or staying far away from me because I was dirty and smelled. I remember meeting with the guidance counselor regularly. She always asked me if everything was okay at home while I would color or do a word search. I always said the same thing. "Everything is fine, I'm doing good." I didn't understand why I kept meeting with her and why she was always asking me about my home life. I thought what was going on as normal. I thought it was just a typical 3rd grader with normal things going on at home. The guidance counselor eventually found out where I had been living and told my mom what was happening and that if she didn't get me out from under their roof, she would have no choice but to get social services involved. My mom did get me out of that environment and that phase of life was over with. She did everything she could to the best of her ability. She tried to provide for me and raise me, but being a single mother trying to make ends meet, it was hard for her. She never could find the right guy either. She would always find herself with someone who was abusive to her either verbally or physically.

Fast forward to my senior year in high school, the man she was with was not a good father figure for me or my younger brother (from a previous marriage). I think I intimidated him because I was 18 at the time, and I guess it bothered his ego to have me around. I would come home from school and my mom would try to avoid me because she didn't want me to see the bruises he left all over her. It put me into a tough position because I truly didn't know what to do. Should I beat this guy up? Should I call the cops? It was very difficult for me because I didn't want to be responsible for bringing more harm to my family. I felt like I was the big issue because that's the vibe he gave off. I had to get out of there with the hope that it would take pressure off of my mother. My 8-year-old brother, with tears in his eyes, helped me pack my book bag with clothes and I left out of the window of my bedroom and walked to my girlfriend's house and lived there until he left my mom. He left her in a bind. The power was off and there was barely any food for her or my brother. I moved back in 2 months before my high-school graduation and got a job at the nearest grocery store to help her with the bills and food. I would get off the school bus, go straight to the store around 3:30, work until 10, come home, and the next day repeated the process. While people at school were focused on getting high scores on their ACT or which college they'd be attending, I was wondering which tv dinner my brother would want to eat that night.

> *"You must tell yourself, "no matter how hard it is, or how hard it gets, I'm going to make it." -Les Brown*

I say all of that for this one very enlightening point. Being positive isn't discrediting reality. Being realistic in the fact that bad things happen is obvious but being positive is being more than just being realistic. It's choosing to look at the bright side even when it's dark. I didn't have the best childhood, but let's be fair, who did? Everyone has a story; you could have had or maybe you are going through a very difficult time in your life. Do everything you can to not let it affect you. You overcame the hardship regardless of how tough it was. Even if you're going through something difficult right now, you are here, you have strength. Look at how much you've gone through and look where you are today. You should be proud! Your past experiences make you strong enough to go through the next hurdle life will throw at you. Being positive is not to assume bad things don't happen and won't happen in the future. Corruption, sickness, and death are real and have affected everyone who has ever lived. To be positive, you have to acknowledge the negative. There is a beautifully put analogy that I stumbled across not too long ago that truly makes me think about life as a whole regarding the way we look at and handle situations. There are two wolves that are battling within each of us. One is evil, full of anger, jealousy, envy, sorrow, doubt, regret, and greed. The other wolf is good. It represents joy, peace, love, abundance, humility, empathy, hope, and generosity. So which wolf wins? the one you feed.

"Once you replace negative thoughts with positive ones, you'll start having positive results." -Willie Nelson

There's a guy that works with me that has to be the most positive person I've ever met. I've been around him every day for about 5 years and I can seriously not remember a time where he's not smiling or laughing at something. I'm not sure exactly how old he is. Probably his mid-70s. He's had heart issues in the past, but he still keeps a smile on his face, all the trials he's faced in his life never holds him down. The hardships don't control his life. He loves fishing whenever he gets a chance. He mentions spending time with his son as often as he can, as the rest of his family. He is happy because he chooses to be happy.

"Positivity always wins...always." -Gary Vaynerchuck

You would never know the struggles he's gone through in his life because of how happy he is and how happy he outwardly expresses himself to everyone. Everything that has ever happened to him has made him the person he is today. He doesn't let his past struggles define the person he is. He decides to be happy. He makes the best out of every opportunity that life throws at him.

> *"There is hope even when your brain tells you there isn't."* -John Greene

Death is the toughest thing to deal with. We all know someone who has died, how much it hurts, and how much we miss them. How can you be positive when you lose someone you love? At first, you don't want to be positive; you just want to hurt. But there does come a time where you have to find a way to continue to live your life happily. That's what they would have wanted. I lost a close friend a couple of months ago. Instead of thinking of him as being gone, I think of all the funny memories we had. I think of all the jokes we'd made. The music he liked. Thinking of the things that remind me of him makes him continue to live on in my memory. Instead of getting sad when thinking about him, I think about the good times, the times that we cherished.

> *"Stay positive and happy. Work hard and don't give up. Be open to criticism and keep learning. Surround yourself with happy genuine people."* -Tena Desae

Applying this chapter to the process of writing this book is how I'm able to even get it done. I might not be the most literate guy when it comes to writing, but that's not going to stop me. I'm giving it my all. I'm doing the best that I can. I'm not focusing on how to come up with the next idea for the next sentence, I'm just going with the flow. I feel that life is very similar, you can't be so concerned with the intricacies and difficulties that there will be. Instead, you have to focus on the positive sides of life. Be happy! You have that choice. To make the most of every opportunity that life presents you. Everything you've been through has made you the person you are today with the mindset you have.

> *"Only in the darkness can you see the stars."* -Martin Luther King Jr.

If I could change what happened in my past, would I do it? Absolutely not. Without every experience, I wouldn't be the exact person I am today writing this for you. So, what if it was tough? I'm here, aren't I? I'm living the best life I can. It's the only life I know how to live. Realistically, without positivity in my mind, I probably would have never even tried to write this book. When I look at all the progress I've made with writing this book, I can use the analogy of a glass that has water filled up to the middle of it. If I think to myself that I still have 7 chapters to write and I ask myself how I am going to keep this up, then it could overwhelm me and make me restless or scared to go on. That mentality is glass half-empty. If I look at how proud I am of myself for writing 7 chapters, it doesn't even come to mind how I will come up with the rest of it. Each passing chapter has been progressing to what will be the end goal. The glass is half-full if I keep this up. As this chapter closes, I have one question for you. How do you see the glass of water in your life? Is the glass half-empty or is it half-full?

CHAPTER 8

---·✦·---

ABUNDANCE AND APPRECIATION

Abundance: A very large quantity of something.

Appreciation: Recognition and enjoyment of the good qualities of someone or something.

FOR MOST PEOPLE, MONEY IS THE dictator of their true happiness in life. My wife and I work full-time jobs so we can provide for our 1-year-old. Money is something we don't have a lot of so, I can't tell you how to find abundance in it. What I can tell you is that we go to the park, out to dinner, or we'll catch a movie. Does not having a lot of money mean you can't be abundant? Not at all. Money doesn't dictate the abundance of love and happiness we have in our hearts, and it doesn't for you.

"Doing what you love is the cornerstone of having abundance in your life." -Wayne Dyer

Is there something wrong with wanting more money to enjoy more things? Of course not, but we can't let that warp our mind from what's important. True abundance is internal. What you find to bring the most out of yourself is the key to finding the abundance in your everyday life. It's an outward expression of viewing what you do have instead of what you don't.

"If you look at what you have in life, YOU'LL ALWAYS HAVE MORE." -Oprah Winfrey

Whenever I start to get stressed or upset, I always think of 3 things that I'm thankful for. You can be thankful for someone you love or a place you love to visit that brings you peace of mind. It can be a song or activity you love to do. It can be anything to get you into a peaceful mindset. Since I've started this experiment with myself, I've noticed a difference in the way I react and respond to the world around me.

"When we are grateful, fear disappears, and abundance appears." -Anthony Robbins

Don't take for granted anything in life because it can disappear as fast as you can snap your fingers. Start realizing how good you have it. There are places in the world where people live in houses made out of mud and walk miles to get water. Regardless of how bad you think you have it, when you look at how fortunate you are for the life you do have, the job you have, and the friends you have, life just starts getting better. Go to work with a smile on your face and be happy you made it. Think of the people that enjoy being around you. Think of how much you mean to them and how much they mean to you. Before long, more things that you find abundance in start gravitating toward you because your attitude has shifted to finding more things to be appreciative of.

"Gratitude creates a positive gravitational field and is that which anchors and attracts the good to the orbit of your life." - Devani Alderson

Have you ever heard of a gratitude journal? In case you haven't, it's a diary for you to write everything you are thankful for in a day. As the days go by, you will start noticing more and more things to be thankful for. It is a good way to shift your mind into realizing that good things happen every single day to you.

> *"Acknowledging the good that you already have in your life is the foundation for all abundance."* - Eckart Tolle

Although it can be tough, you have to be appreciative of the abundance you do have in your life. It's the centerpiece to gaining more satisfaction in your own heart and receiving more things to be appreciative of having. Let's say that you want to go get some fast food, but you only have a few bucks to spare. Be thankful for the dollar menu.

> *"Whatever you appreciate and give thanks for will increase in your life."* - Sanaya Roman

As I wrap this chapter up, I want to emphasize how important it is that I have gratitude in my own life. I'm thankful to understand that I have the choice to be appreciative of the abundance I have in my life. Step outside; take a deep breath of the fresh air. See how beautiful the trees are. If the sun is shining, think about how it's bringing life to everything you can see. If it's raining, think of how rain is the way the flowers and the trees get their strength. Abundance is all around you, but only if you allow it within you.

CHAPTER 9

·•◎•·

MEDITATE

Meditate: think deeply or focus one's mind for a while, in silence or with the aid of chanting, for religious or spiritual purposes or as a method of relaxation.

M EDITATING HAS BECOME SUCH AN IMPORTANT part of my life. It's time I set aside to strengthen myself; to enhance anything that I want to focus on. It is highly effective at controlling anxiety and reducing stress.

"The quieter you become, the more you can hear." -Baba Ram Dass

Have you ever wondered how many thoughts run through an average person's mind a day? It's roughly between 60,000 and 80,000 per day. How many of them are you solely responsible for? Are you controlling them or are they controlling you? Some of them could be pointless negativity or regrets that we just can't let go of. Thoughts that are not helping ourselves or anyone around in the slightest. I would constantly think about anything and everything to beat myself up over. Things that were so insignificant to my daily routine. I would critique every little thing I could think of about myself. Creating paranoia for no reason. I've wasted so much time misusing the most powerful tool we have, the mind.

"The thing about meditation is, you become more and more you." -David Lynch

Since I've started meditating daily, I can't stop. I can't believe how much control I now have over myself. Every aspect of my life I'm viewing completely different because of meditation.

> *"The goal of meditation isn't to control your thoughts, it's to stop letting them control you."* - Jon Andre

If you don't already meditate, I would strongly recommend that you start. It can reduce physical pain, increase the body's immune system, and give you more energy. Meditation helps reduce heart disease, increases blood flow, slows heart rate, and provides a sense of calm, peace and balance. It is a way for us to help ourselves.

> *"Calmness of mind is one of the beautiful jewels of wisdom."* - James Allen

Meditation has helped me continue my journey in this book. All of the ideas that I've written down come from deep within my mind. I've been able to express all of the chapters in my own words. I wouldn't have been able to find the right things to say otherwise. Meditation has kept my mind focused on more important things in my own life as well. I've been reaping the benefits of calmness with productivity. I've reaped quicker results of personal growth with my new-found peace of mind.

> *"Quiet the mind and the soul will speak."* - Ma Jaya Sati Bhagavati

Meditation has given me the right things to say at the right time in each chapter up until this point. To not overthink what I will write next, but to let it flow from within. I will continue to use this phenomenal gift to finish what I've started with this book and whatever life brings my way. Through mediation, I've become sound in mind and have control of my thoughts. May this information about meditation be implemented and helpful in your everyday life as I couldn't imagine life without it in mine.

CHAPTER 10

---·•◦✸◦•·---

SUCCESS

Success: the accomplishment of an aim or purpose.

Look at how far I've come! Momentum has taken over and it's all smooth sailing from here. I cannot be stopped, nor will I give in. I'm on the 10th chapter of a book built to help us achieve our dreams and put our best foot forward with inspiration from everything that has been presented to both of us. I would say we are succeeding.

> *"All successful people have a goal. No one can get anywhere unless he knows where he wants to go and what he wants to be or do."* - Norman Vincent Peale

You are the epitome of success. If you are alive right now, you are succeeding. Take full advantage of the opportunity you have right now to go after what you've set yourself up for: success.

> *"Self-belief and hard work will always earn you success."* - Virat Kohli

All your trials and tribulations have made you a strong and wise individual. With all of that experience under your belt, you have the necessary tools to succeed in whatever challenge you take on. There is nothing that you cannot do.

> *"Behind every successful man, there's a lot of unsuccessful years."* - Bob Brown

Steve Jobs started in his garage. Steve Harvey lived in his car for 3 years. Walt Disney declared bankruptcy just a year after opening his company. Jim Carrey lived in a van and had to quit school when he was just 15 to work as a janitor. Oprah Winfrey lived in poverty and was neglected and abused. You may be no different from exactly where they were at their lowest points. They give me confidence in that I'm right where I need to be. I've weathered the storm; I am the diamond in the rough. I'm not only built for success, but destined for it, and so are you.

> *"Success is not what you have, but who you are."* -Bo Bennett

There was a legendary basketball coach by the name of John Wooden that described success beautifully. He said: "Success is peace of mind, which is a direct result of self-satisfaction in knowing you did your best to become the best you are capable of being."

No matter how much you achieve, you can always strive for more. There is always room to grow. You aren't done until you're the best you can be.

> *"Success isn't always about greatness. It's about consistency. Consistent hard work leads to success. Greatness will come."* -Dwayne Johnson

Don't say I want to be successful; say I AM successful. Whatever you are working on, whatever you are doing, I don't care what it is. Do it to the best of your ability. If you're a receptionist, be the best receptionist you can be. If you're a salesman, be the best salesman you can be. If you're a beet farmer, be the best dang beet farmer you can be.

> *"Action is the foundational key to all success."* - Pablo Picasso

I consider myself successful. My mind is where it needs to be, constantly pushing myself for excellence. I'm responsible for where I am, and where I'm going. Every day is a new day to work harder than the day before. There are no limitations. The only limitation that can hold me back from greatness is me.

> *"There are no secrets to success. It is the result of preparation, hard work, and learning from failure."* - Colin Powell

Are you successful? If you say yes, then you have and will achieve whatever you have your heart set on. If you say no, then you never will be. Don't look at your feet, look at the stars. Keep your eyes on the prize. If you have the mindset for success, then you're already successful.

> *"The secret of success in life is for a man to be ready for his opportunity when it comes."* - Benjamin Disraeli

As my journey continues, I must appreciate how far I've come and keep in mind how much farther I have yet to go. I've been climbing this mountain of destiny and can see so much that I never imagined I would. If you're at the bottom of this imaginary mountain or right by my side, this quest for inspiration, excellence, and self-gratification doesn't stop here; we have to keep going. We have so much we still haven't accomplished. May you always understand you are a living breathing success unless of course you don't want to be.

CHAPTER 11

—————— •❈• ——————

ADVENTURE

Adventure: an unusual and exciting, typically hazardous experience or activity.

D O YOU LIKE TO TRAVEL TO places you've never been to? Have you ever taken a road trip to see just where you would end up; just to see things you never thought you would? To live a little, and to treat yourself to new experiences?

"If happiness is the goal, and it should be then adventures should be a top priority." -Richard Branson

Starting an adventure may be a difficult thing to do. Now, granted, it can be intimidating not knowing what to expect. You don't know what type of people you will run into along the way, and you might just want to stay right where you are in your cozy little bubble where nothing will ever change. Let me ask: how is that going for you?

"If it scares you, it might be a good thing to try." -Seth Godin

You need to hear this just like I do, life is fleeting. Within a second it could be gone. Soon it will be gone. Make the most of every opportunity you have right now to live and enjoy your life. Meet new people, do things you've never done, go to places you've never been to. My friend, what do you have to lose?

"Adventure is worthwhile." - Aristotle

There's one account that has made me start thinking of the way I treat life differently. Wayne Dyer was a professor at a university in New York where he had written 3 textbooks for the school. They offered him a tenure to have a guaranteed job as a professor for the rest of his life. While he was driving home, he pulled off the side of the road and started contemplating if he should accept it. The way he described his decision is phenomenal. He said to himself "Am I going to live for 90 years or am I going to live 1 year 90 times?". He wound up turning down the offer, and after that, he lived the best life he could imagine for himself.

> *"The biggest adventure you can ever take is to live the life of your dreams."* - Oprah Winfrey

I hope to go from coast to coast one day to see all of the things I've only ever seen in pictures and movies. To enjoy every minute of every hour that I have. To not be irresponsible, of course, but to be in complete control of where I am and where I'm going. Not to let others bring me down along the way, but to build them up as I go. To encourage them to live their lives.

> *"I hope you never stop seeing the world. Even when your eyes are closed."* - Rashiki

Think about how many movies you've watched that is predicated around an adventure. The "hero's journey" if you will. You are the hero of your journey. Go out and live it! You'll have your own stories to tell about how beautiful the world is and how much fun you had exploring it. You are the star and the director. The cameras are rolling, what are you going to do?

> *"I always wonder why birds stay in the same place when they can fly anywhere on earth. Then I ask myself the same question."* - Harun Yahya

Have you ever asked yourself what do you truly want out of your life?

Have you ever looked inside yourself and pondered that? We think too little of ourselves to try new things. We are afraid we might look silly dancing to no music or laughing to no joke. There is nothing wrong with being different. Stand out! Shock others and yourself! Be spontaneous! You are the only you there is!

> *"The world is big, and I want to have a good look at it before it gets dark."* - John Muir

As I continue on this adventure within this book, it makes me understand how important our lives truly are. One day we will wake up and look back on everything we've done and said to ourselves "Where did all the time go?" I will feel like I was in my 20s just yesterday and I will not let my life pass me by. Will I have the same story to tell my kids and grandkids over and over or will I have countless stories from so many different places, that I'll never be able to convey every one of them? It's only too late to start an adventure when your adventure comes to an end. Think about that.

CHAPTER 12

· •❊• ·

LOVE

Love: an intense feeling of deep affection.

FEBRUARY 6ᵀᴴ, 2016, I REMEMBER PRECISELY the moment where my closest friend came down the aisle to meet my hand in marriage. I instantly broke out into tears. Fast forward to October 15ᵗʰ, 2018, I recall running back and forth down the hall to get ice chips for my wife, putting a cold rag on her head, giving an oxygen mask to her, and then watched as she gave birth to our baby boy. Those days were the two happiest days of my life.

"You always gain by giving love." - Reese Witherspoon

I have sincerely loved writing this book for you. It's a way that I can show you how much I appreciate and love you. Maybe you're going through a period in your life where you're not receiving love, or just don't want it. You might not be getting the affection you deserve and need. Know that you are loved. You are a special person and should always keep their head up and just keep going no matter what life has thrown at you. I believe in you. You can do it.

"You can't blame gravity for falling in love." - Albert Einstein

Love is the most powerful force because it has no limits. Love makes us do crazy things. It makes us look like a fool to get attention. It makes us travel far distances just to see someone smile. Love might just make us write a poem, a song, or a book.

> *"' I love you'" means that I accept you for the person that you are, and I don't wish to change you into someone else. It means that I do not expect perfection from you just as you don't expect it from me. 'I love you' means that I love you and stand by you even through the worst of times. It means loving you when you are in a bad mood or too tired to do the things that I want to do. It means loving you when you are down, not just when your fun to be with."* - Deanne Laura Gilbert

In school, I failed in both language and writing. To be honest this is more out of my comfort zone than anything I've ever done. So, knowing that from the popular opinion I'm wasting my time, why would I do it? It's because I needed this, I needed to write this and read it. I care deeply and I love who I am. The person I am has a destiny to fulfill and it starts with loving myself.

Once I've understood how to love myself, then I can express that love to everyone I come in contact with in-person or through this book.

> *"Only one life, that soon is past. Only what's done with love will last."* - Unknown

To think on deeper matters of how one day we will be a distant memory can shake someone to their core. If it's all for nothing, what's this life for? When I'm gone and the people that knew me are gone. I no longer exist, at least from human consciousness. That's deep. So why would I do this? What's the point? Love triumphs everything and is the MOST powerful force in the universe. With my love for people, I've managed to write this in the best way I could. I hope you truly get the point of my message in these pages. You are the most amazing person that there is. Have love in your heart for yourself, the ones you hold dear, your enemies, your accomplishments, your failures, your past, and your future.

> *"The best and most beautiful things in the world cannot be seen or even heard but must be felt with the heart."* -Helen Keller

As I continue this ever-fleeting journey, I have come to accept and love myself more and more. I know that I'm making a difference in the world with love. With compassion and genuine love, I've been pouring my heart out into these pages. Together we have come so far to give up on ourselves and our loved ones. Our journey isn't over, and with love, our journey never truly ends

CHAPTER 13

.•⊛•.

INSPIRATION

Inspiration: the process of being mentally stimulated to
do or feel something, especially to do something creative

THIS ENTIRE BOOK'S SOLE PURPOSE IS to inspire. To inspire me, the
author, to write it. To inspire me to chase after my dreams and
continue to find happiness in my life. This book's ultimate purpose is
to inspire you to be the best person you can be for yourself. To help you
find happiness and your own path. Not to let destiny control you, but for
you to control your own destiny. Take a brief second from reading if you
will. Close your eyes and take 3 deep breaths. Open your eyes and take in
the reality that you are existing right now. At this moment you are alive.
You are a conscious human being; thinking your own thoughts. Think
about how appreciative you are at this moment. Do not think of the past,
and do not think of the future. Right now is all we have. Be thankful for
everything you have right now because, within a second, it could/will all
be gone. Don't take your life for granted. Instead, use it to inspire you,
which in turn, will inspire others.

*"Sometimes you will never know the value of a moment until
it becomes a memory."* -Dr. Seuss

Everything I've said so far has been for us to grow. To develop our
minds into going after what we want before it's too late. None of your
friends, colleagues, or members of your family have control of the life you

decide to live. Don't worry about what others might say about the path you want to follow. Don't worry about the path that they are choosing or the path that they want you to follow. It's none of your business what they do with their life and vice-versa. Your life is yours for a reason. You have a purpose, I promise; all it takes is effort and dedication to finding what that purpose is.

> *"Surround yourself with people who are only going to lift you higher."* - Oprah Winfrey

Everything you've ever done has put you right here in this moment. To succeed and thrive. To beat the odds and surpass all limitations. To prove your worth to yourself and everyone who doubts you. YOU ARE HERE. Why would you stop now? I will NEVER give up on you! Don't you dare give up on yourself!

I am inspiring those who want to be inspired. No one can stop me because I've already done it. I've overcome everything that has ever been thrown at me, and it's brought me to this moment where I'm encouraging you to go after your own dreams and ambitions so that your ideas will build a better world and change history forever as we know it.

> *"Instead of letting your hardships and failures discourage or exhaust you, let them inspire you."* - Michelle Obama

We all have stories to tell. Stories about things that we've gone through in our life and the person that it has made us become. Use those stories as fuel to light your fire of determination, and let it drive you to your destination. Find anything and everything to motivate you to get you to the top of your mountain.

> *"Try to be a rainbow in someone's cloud."* -Maya Angelo

As this book nears its end, I've appreciated everything that has brought me to this point. I've inspired myself to keep going and to never look back. I'm so proud of myself and the accomplishments I've made along the way. No matter what, I've made a difference in at least one person's life, mine.

I've come a long way. I used to not want to do anything with my life, but now, I'm inspiring everyone that wants a better life for themselves. Look at you. You have been along for this ride of inspiration. How does it make you view your life? Do you cherish it more? Are you satisfied with the direction your heading? If I've been any help, then this book is serving its purpose.

CHAPTER 14

————— ·•⊛•· —————

FINISH

Finish: bring (a task or activity) to an end; complete.

I'VE SET OUT AND ACCOMPLISHED WHAT I started. I've started so many things in the past just to give up on them at a later time. It took courage for me to put the effort into writing a book about self-help and inspiration not only for me but for you. Courage for me to show you that you can start right now.

"Many will start fast; few will finish strong." - Gary Ryan Blair

My dream is to inspire you to chase your dreams. I want you to go after what you want in life with all of your heart. Do NOT let anyone tell you can't achieve your dreams. Show them you will. I'm chasing mine, and through my pursuit, I am changing the world right now. I'm impacting my everyday life by dreaming bigger than I ever thought I could. I fully believe that I will inspire the world. I will change the course of history forever as did the great historians of the past. I believe that we will make the world a better place. Believe in yourself. Never doubt who you are, and no one else ever will.

"Finished last, will always be better than did not finish, which always trumps did not start." - Unknown

Goals are things we will always be able to accomplish if we set them. My goal has been to convey this book the best way that I know how to. Make sure you set goals for yourself. Goals that you know you can do and ones you don't know if you can do because, either way, you can achieve them. It's taken a lot of humility for me to recognize my regrets and failures in order to become a better person. You can't learn from your mistakes if you don't own up to them. You will never reach a point in your life where you're too big to be humbled. Keep that close in mind, and never forget it.

> *"Have enough courage to start, and enough heart to finish."* - Jessica N. S. Yourko

Leadership is standing up for what you believe in. Even in the face of persecution, always be courageous. Lead by example, and never forget the best leaders knew who to follow and how to do it. Do ALL things with a positive attitude. Regardless of how bad your past might be, today is a new day. Bad things happen to everyone, pick up the pieces and move on from it. This isn't a perfect world, but we can perfect the way we view it.

> *"Starting strong is good. Finishing strong is epic."* - Robin Sharma

Abundance and appreciation go hand in hand. Be appreciative of the things you have in life, and you will start noticing how much you truly have. You should be thankful as soon as you wake up the next morning, as you know it isn't promised. Meditate regularly to find inner peace. It has helped me in more ways than I ever assumed. You will not regret trying it.

> *"A ferocious concentration and fanatical execution are what you need to finish strong."* - Gary Ryan Blair

Don't say, "I want to be successful." You already are. Never stop chasing what's rightfully yours.

Success isn't measured by one man's achievements; success is measured by one man's will to achieve. Writing this has been an adventure for me. It reminds me that this is my life to live. I will see the world and meet many people before it's all said and done. The question is, will you?

"To finish first, you must first finish." - Rick Mears

Love with all that you have. Give everything you have into your next step. I have your back, I believe in you, never stop loving who you are at your core.

I hope I've been an inspiration to you because I have inspired myself to do more than just write this book. I will go out and reach those that need the motivation to believe in themselves and chase after their purpose the way I'm chasing mine.

Inspiration comes from within. You have to inspire yourself before you can inspire others.

The time is now. I've given you all that I can. With my words and the best quotes that I could find to get my point across and further my purpose. My pursuit of this book is complete. I couldn't have done it without you. My love for you chasing your destiny is the reason why I decided to do this in the first place. My calling is to help you, by doing that, I helped myself. I am forever grateful for you and will always be here to support you. Even when I'm gone, you can always go back and read this. As you make your way through life and create the future you want, think about how you can help someone while doing so. Your dreams will come true when it's centered around inspiring others, for you were destined to inspire. Thank you.

"Whether you think you can or think you can't, you're right." - Henry Ford